How Many Flamingos Tall Is a Giraffe?

CREATIVE WAYS TO LOOK AT HEIGHT

by Clara Cella

PEBBLE
a capstone imprint

Let's measure a giraffe, head to toes, using some plastic pink flamingos!

The giraffe is 7 flamingos tall!

It's someone's birthday! Grab a fork! How many **cakes** are as tall as a stork?

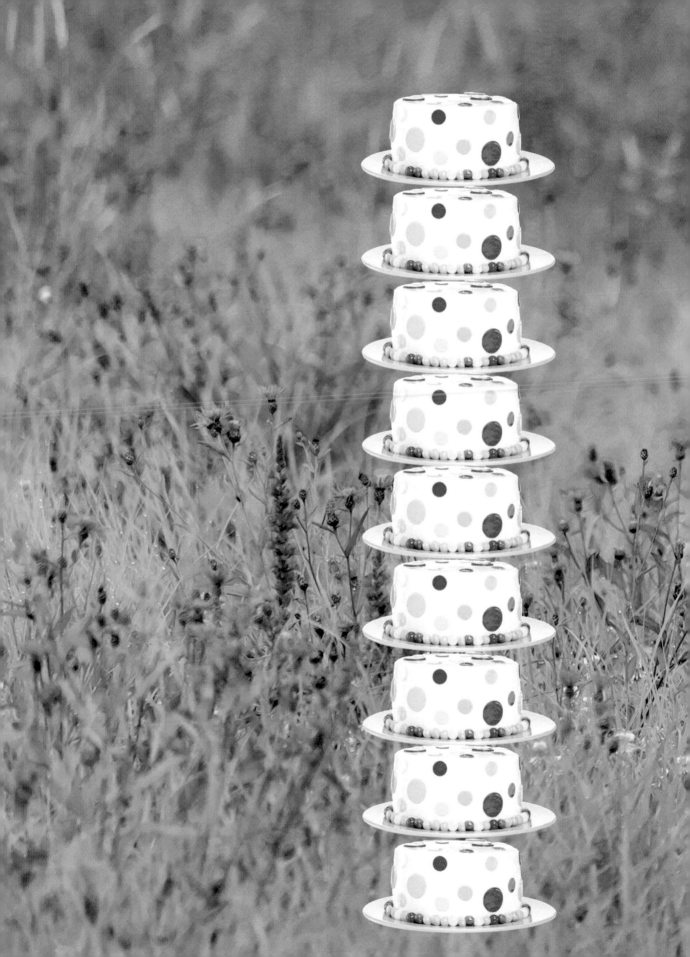

9 cakes!

To measure the height of this great **pup**, let's use dog toys. Add them up!

How many
ladybugs,
spotted and small,
equal the height
of one tennis ball?

20 ladybugs!

Measuring a snowman is a bit of a trick. He's melting fast! Better be quick!

The snowman is 11 birds tall!

Get ready!
Get set!
Alley-OOP!
How many
pumpkins tall is
the **hoop**?

12 pumpkins!

How many elephants equal the height of one monster truck that is ready to bite?

1 elephant!

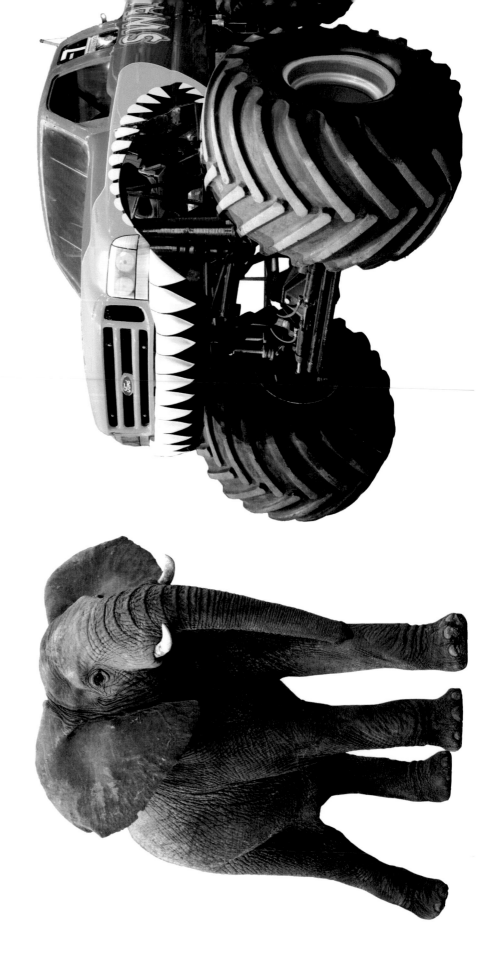

LOOK FOR OTHER BOOKS IN THE SERIES:

How Many Ducks Could Fit in a Bus?

CREATIVE WAYS TO LOOK AT VOLUME
by Clara Cella

How Many Kittens Could Ride a Shark?

CREATIVE WAYS TO LOOK AT LENGTH
by Clara Cella

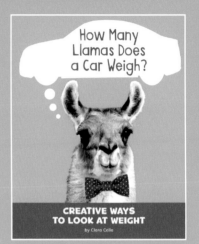

How Many Llamas Does a Car Weigh?

CREATIVE WAYS TO LOOK AT WEIGHT
by Clara Cella

Pebble Sprout is published by Pebble, an imprint of Capstone.

1710 Roe Crest Drive, North Mankato, Minnesota 56003

www.capstonepub.com

Library of Congress Cataloging-in-Publication Data

Names; Cella, Clara, author. Title; How many flamingos tall is a giraffe?; creative ways to look at height / by Clara Cella. Description; North Mankato, Minnesota ; Pebble, [2020] | Series; Silly measurements | Audience; Ages 4-6 | Audience; Grades K-1 | Summary; Flamingos, jack-o'-lanterns, and six other fun, non-standard measuring units demonstrate the math concept of height. Through the use of whimsical composite photos and a hint of text, pre-readers learn the height of a giraffe, a snowman, a tennis ball, and more;— Provided by publisher. Identifiers: LCCN 2019043922 (print) | LCCN 2019043923 (ebook) | ISBN 9781977113221 (hardcover) | ISBN 9781977120090 (paperback) | ISBN 9781977113269 (pdf) Subjects; LCSH; Altitudes—Measurement—Juvenile literature. Classification; LCC QC90.6 .C45 2020 (print) | LCC QC90.6 (ebook) | DDC 530.8—dc23 LC record available at https;//lccn.loc.gov/2019043922 LC ebook record available at https;//lccn.loc.gov/2019043923

Image Credits

Shutterstock: Alexander Raths, 28 (angry grinning pumpkin), 29, cynoclub, 12 (hedgehog dog toy), David Gilder, 12–13 (backyard), Denis Tabler, 21 (ladybug), EFKS, 27, Eivaisla, 5 (flamingo), Ellie.tuang, 20–21 (tennis court), Eric Isselee, 11, 12–13 (dog), Four Oaks, 31 (elephant), Gemenacom, 15, 17, Hiromi Ito Ame, 4–5 (back), Joanna Zopoth-Lipiejko, 19, Ju Jae-young, 17 (hedgehog), Kurt Adams, cover (flamingo), 1, Ljupco Smokovski, 7, 8, Lotus_studio, 3, Maglara, 16–17 (back), Mark Herreid, 28–29 (outdoor basketball hoop), MMCez, 8–9 (back), Pavel L Photo and Video, 31 (monster truck), photofort 77, cover (top), back cover, siaminka, cover (monocle), 1, Smit, 23, 24–25 (back), xpixel, 25 (bird), Yellowj, 28 (pumpkin with sharp teeth and happy pumpkin), 29

Editorial Credits

Editor: Jill Kalz; Designer: Ted Williams; Media Researcher: Svetlana Zhurkin; Production Specialist: Katy LaVigne

Printed in the United States   5004